PAIGN

Chips Barber
and
Sally Barber

GW00542702

Best wishes!
Chips Barber

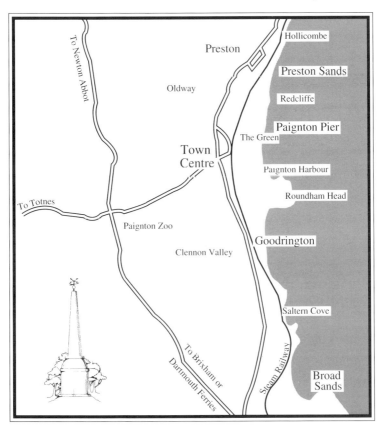

Hollicombe
Preston
Preston Sands
To Newton Abbot
Oldway
Redcliffe
Paignton Pier
The Green
Town Centre
Paignton Harbour
Roundham Head
To Totnes
Paignton Zoo
Goodrington
Clennon Valley
Saltern Cove
To Brixham or Dartmouth Ferries
Steam Railway
Broad Sands

OBELISK PUBLICATIONS

ALSO BY THE AUTHOR
Around & About the Haldon Hills
The Lost City of Exeter
Diary of a Dartmoor Walker
Diary of a Devonshire Walker
The Great Little Dartmoor Book
The Great Little Exeter Book
Made in Devon (with David FitzGerald)
Dartmoor in Colour
Burgh Island & Bigbury Bay (with Judy Chard)
Dark & Dastardly Dartmoor (with Sally Barber)
Exeter in Colour / Torbay in Colour
The Ghosts of Exeter (with Sally Barber)
The Great Little Totnes Book
Tales of the Teign (with Judy Chard)
Ten Family Walks on Dartmoor (with Sally Barber)
The Great Little Plymouth Book
Plymouth in Colour
Weird & Wonderful Dartmoor (with Sally Barber)
Ghastly & Ghostly Devon (with Sally Barber)
Dawlish & Dawlish Warren
The South Hams
Brixham
Torquay

OTHER TITLES ABOUT THIS AREA INCLUDE:
Walking "with a Tired Terrier" In and Around Torbay, Brian Carter
The Ghosts of Torbay, Deryck Seymour
The Ghosts of Brixham, Graham Wyley
Peter Tully's Pictures of Paignton, Parts I and II

For further details of any of our titles, please contact us at the address below or
telephone Exeter (0392) 68556

Sketch map on title page by Sally Barber
Photographs by or belonging to Chips Barber
Drawings on page 4 (top) and page 8 by Jane Reynolds

First published in 1992 by
Obelisk Publications, 2 Church Hill, Pinhoe, Exeter, Devon
Designed by Chips and Sally Barber
Typeset by Sally Barber
Printed in Great Britain by Sprint Print, Okehampton Place, Exeter

Paignton

There are millions of people all over Britain who will know Paignton as the place where they spent a memorable holiday. They will remember the vivid red sands and cliffs, the wide open spaces, the pier, the amusements, and the railway. The chances are they will look on the Devonshire resort with a great deal of fondness as it has given so many people so much pleasure. Paignton has played host to the famous, has accommodated the masses and survived to be the acknowledged family resort of Torbay. It has been bracketed with its larger neighbour of Torquay to the north and its smaller bedfellow of Brixham to the south since 1968. Sandwiched between them Paignton is not at all pretentious, it is a good honest resort to which people return time after time. But how many of those people have gone home without knowing anything of the town's past or heritage? In this little book we will look at what it is that makes Paignton the place it is today.

All towns have a history (and hopefully a future) but not all towns can boast a history as long as Paignton's! It is almost thirteen centuries since a Saxon called Paega wandered onto the scene in this part of Tor Bay. He was the religious leader of a small group looking for a suitable site on which to set up his church and to develop his agricultural community. Quite possibly at that time there was a lagoon somewhere between what is now Paignton Beach and the base of the inland hills. Paega set up his settlement, and developed his farm or 'ton', on a dry shelf of red sandstone above it. In his wildest dreams, the man responsible for 'Paega's ton' would never have envisaged the Paignton we know today!

Not a lot is known about the small religious community of Saxon origin but later, in Norman times, it was decided that the site was good enough to merit a manor!

The canny worldly-wise fourteenth century Bishops of Exeter also had an eye for a good spot – well away from the madding crowds with the fevers, epidemics and diseases that they harboured. The incumbent bishop could freely hunt deer in the extensive woodlands that existed

where the heavily developed residential area of Polsham and Preston are today.

One of the oldest areas of Paignton is around Church Street and Winner Street, previously called Wynerde Street or Vineyard Street. The suitability of the soils, the sheltered aspect of the site, and the generally sunny south facing slopes were ideal for the growing of grapes. In later years Paignton developed a considerable reputation as a cider and cabbage producer.

Roundham Head was important as it provided the ideal location for a jetty. The headland gave excellent protection for such a construction to tuck snugly under the north side of its deep red cliffs. The manor had been established half a mile inland and to reach it a raised path above the marshes was constructed to give access. This route was originally called Fisher Street and remained so until Victorian times when it was renamed Sands Road. The track also bridged a gap between the two existing settlements – the coastal Paignton Quay and the inland Paignton Well – as the town developed.

At Paignton Well farming, crafts, accommodation and trade

occupied the population, whereas at the coast the pursuits were naturally of a maritime disposition. The gently shelved beaches were ideal for seine fishermen to practice their piscatorial pursuits. Continued healthy catches beyond Tudor times assured Paignton Quay of a thriving existence and, by the mid-seventeenth century, a number of substantial buildings occupied the site.

The southern end of Paignton Green was originally foreshore where nets were mended or dried—an old privilege still held today. The port officer for the Quay had the splendid title 'Guardianus de les keys' and his tenants all received half an acre of land to use as a fish market.

However, as men went further afield to catch fish, Paignton Quay declined in prosperity. Reports in the early nineteenth century indicated that the pier was ruinous, and that the jetty itself was in need of great attention. In about 1839 major work was carried out and the little port flourished for another century until Paignton Harbour again receded into poor fortunes in the 1930s.

The council bought the harbour and gave it a facelift. Alas their undoubted good intentions earned scathing criticism from several quarters. The atmosphere of the old harbour had disappeared—according to locals. One description said that it was "a hybrid cross between a car park and a film set, except that the gaudy booking huts on the north quay impart a soupçon of fair-ground atmosphere". Typical of the changes wrought was the conversion of a Coastguard building into public conveniences. This photograph shows it as it was in 1910.

Paignton Harbour can at least claim one unique distinction. In 1936 Miss Stella Gale was appointed as Harbour Master, a post she held for six years. She was the first woman to hold such a post in Great Britain. Although she relinquished the post in 1942 it was kept in the family as her father became the next Harbour Master. The harbour continues to give a lot of people much pleasure, from those who 'mess around in boats' to those who sit and spectate.

The fishing industry at Paignton has all but died, apart from the catching of

visitors for fishing trips. Ticket-selling kiosks are a form of bait alongside the harbour, assuring the boat owners of a more reliable, but non-edible, kind of catch.

The inland community of Paignton Well developed rapidly during Victoria's reign. In the distant Midlands and North of England, mill owners and speculators made a killing from the output of the Industrial Revolution. Many of these people needed an outlet for their vast profits, so what better place to turn but to the South Coast where resorts were beginning to develop? Typical of this was a businessman, called Fletcher, from Birmingham who in 1865 bought a large parcel of land between the railway and sea, much of it swamp land and therefore not too expensive. The land was ripe for development, and Mr Fletcher made another fortune by building villa residences for the ever increasing multitude of wealthy persons migrating to Tor Bay.

Allied to the population growth, the town's shopping facilities increased correspondingly. The original shopping centre, in Winner Street and Church Street, could not cater for the amount of traders wanting to capitalise on this situation. The land between this area and the station was agricultural land, the heartland of the famous Paignton Cabbage, but not sufficiently protected to prevent the developers covering it with Palace Avenue and Victoria Street.

Even the extensive marshes were drained as the rush was on to create a large, important and fashionable resort. At the turn of the century three large hotels were erected, The Esplanade, the Redcliffe and the Gerston. The Esplanade Hotel carried these words in its advertisement: "The climate of Paignton is found to agree with invalids for whom that of Torquay is too relaxing".

In 1923 Mr Hunter-Joy, chairman of the Paignton Chamber of Trade said of Paignton's climate: "In its climate Paignton shares the favours of all South Devon – mild winters, phenomenally early springs and the warmest and brightest summer sunshine to be found in England. Its situation at the head of Torbay not only makes the outlook but assists in making a congenial and healthy climate for while sheltered on both sides by the cliffs of Berry Head and the high hills of

Torquay, Paignton has a broad frontage on the open sea."

Out of a town of 15,000 people, in the early 1920s, only 25 people were unemployed! Everywhere buildings were going up.

Paignton had arrived, but at what cost? The lowlands had been built over and, during the inter-war period, still the demand for more land grew. The builders were forced onto the hills and the green slopes, which had, until now, provided a colourful backcloth. Soon these became covered with a labyrinth of avenues and roads, largely for the 'middle class' type of person. Modest dwellings, in carefully aligned roads, crane over each other for a glimpse of the sea. Paignton has spread right across the hills: one wonders how far it will go. It is not surprising that distant villages like Marldon show concern. Paignton has about 30,000 residents but seen from the air gives the impression of being much bigger. The illusion is caused by the great number of bungalows which only house small households.

In the following pages we will see how Paignton's coastline has become the playground of thousands, and we will discover many of its secrets and the stories which it has to tell. Let's take a north-south journey through this celebrated resort.

There are few places in the county which reflect 'Red Devon' better than Hollicombe Beach. Here the cliffs are so deep red they seem as if they have been painted by man rather than nature. Above on the main road, between Paignton and Torquay, is the gas works, started in 1861. It had originally been intended to put a gasworks on Oddicombe Beach at Babbacombe but the great Isambard Kingdom Brunel was greatly opposed to such an idea. Consequently an Act of Parliament was passed which prevented any such installation being allowed in St. Marychurch or Torquay. The site at Hollicombe was the nearest available site where it could be built, well away from Mr Brunel's territory! This is a much less conspicuous blot on the landscape now because, thanks to North Sea Gas, two large gas holders, between the road and railway, have been replaced by attractive ponds and landscaped grounds.

Access to the beach is through a tunnel beneath the railway. Its lack of facilities tends to keep the visitors, who prefer beaches with more amenities, away. Now it is used mainly by locals although, in the past, even they avoided Hollicombe at certain times because of the proximity of the gasworks. Not only did these shade the beach with their bulk in the afternoons, but also the mountains of coal needed by them often turned the water jet black!

Older Torbay residents might remember the long railway tunnel from which trains emerged to gaze down onto the sea at Hollicombe. Locals called it Gasworks Tunnel but it was also called Hollicombe Tunnel by Paigntonians and Livermead Tunnel by Torquay folk.

The drawing shows a derailment at Hollicombe which happened on 21 September 1866. The 09.53 Kingswear to Paddington train ran off the tracks as

a result of a breakdown in the signalling system. Fortunately nobody was hurt.

Another exciting event the tunnel witnessed was caused by the instability of the sandstone coastline. On 3 February 1903, Mr Bonning, a railway employee, noticed a landslip at Hollicombe Gasworks. Aware of the imminent arrival of the 10:49 from Torquay, he sprinted into the tunnel and just managed to warn the train in time!

In 1908 it was decided that, because of the increase in rail traffic to Paignton, it was necessary to double the track. This meant that the tunnel had to be demolished and a wider cutting made.

Preston Cliffs, or Hollicombe Head, was the scene of an unusual conflict in 1928. A dispute, over public access across the headland, arose between Mr Sidney George Baultwood and wife against Paignton UDC. The council claimed a right of way between Seaway Road and the direction of Torquay. However, coastal erosion meant that an inland detour was necessary and Mr Baultwood's fence was pulled down . . . and then put up . . . and then pulled down . . . 28 times!

The court case, which normally would have been a dull affair, was greatly enriched by the very determined council who went to great lengths to produce a most impressive model of the headland, complete with green flags to mark the route, railing, trees, grass, and even members of the public, all to scale. I'm afraid that I didn't discover the outcome of the case, but I do know that the fence which was taken down was put up yet again and the clifftop site was the scene of scuffles, with punches being thrown as well as pepper. Obviously a heated argument!

An interesting fact, recorded in newspapers at the time, is that Hollicombe was used for rifle practice. A target was placed at the foot of the cliff and two men, at either end of the cliff path, gave warning if members of the public approached.

Because the cliffs at Hollicombe are of soft red rocks, over recent decades they have been wearing back at an alarming rate. Older locals recount that, between the railway line and the sea, there was once a much larger area of grassland One man grew vegetables on part of it. This land must have been the property of the Great Western Railway as they clearly marked the extent of their territory by placing posts, bearing GWR, all around it. Some of these markers were even placed in the sea!

In summer tidy rows of beach huts appear like pearly teeth along the Marine Parade and Preston Green promenade. After a winter of hibernation, this part of Paignton slowly comes to life again. Preston Green provides the perfect space for toddlers to play and for daddies to show off their skills at ball games. How different this scene must have been years ago when young troops were trained here, in trench warfare, ready for First World War action. This photo was taken in about 1877 and shows a new sea wall which has stood the test of time well.

Following these improvements to the coastline, the Redcliffe Estate eyed the possibility of erecting fourteen houses along Preston Green, an idea which would have created a much narrower Marine Drive. However this did not materialise and, a few years afterwards, Paris Singer built an elaborate aeroplane hangar there. These hangars stored three sea planes which took visitors on trips around the bay, after the First World War, for 25 shillings. The planes were lowered down the slipway (near the present cafe on Preston Green), and taxied along to Paignton Pier, where passengers climbed aboard for their short flights.

In December 1920, following the cessation of hostilities during the Great War, two German destroyers were towed up the Channel to Teignmouth to be scrapped. During a storm, they broke loose from the tugs towing them, both washing up onto the Paignton coastline. One went aground at Roundham, whilst the other was beached at Preston. Attempts to get the latter off were thwarted, so the boat was cut in half and the rear end was hauled away. The remaining portion became a local landmark and 'rusted in peace' for several years until scrap metal merchants removed it.

In 1920 when Preston Green was eventually flattened, filled and rolled, it was for recreational reasons. Tennis courts were built and from 1922 cars were allowed to park on the green. This situation remained until 1936. The cafe (Sandy Corner), which was built at the onset of the Second World War, still retains its art deco period appearance.

The most prominent architectural feature along this stretch of coastline is an unusual looking building which would probably be better suited to India than to the end of Paignton Sands. This thought is not entirely misplaced for the building's origins and roots bear more than a pinch of oriental flavouring!

Smith's Folly, as it is frequently called, was the brainchild of the brilliant, but somewhat eccentric, Colonel Robert Smith, born in 1787 in France. At the age of 16 he enlisted with the East India Company's army, the start of a long attachment with India, a place he loved.

Greatly skilled, Robert used his talents as an architect, artist and engineer to design and construct roads, bridges, houses and even palaces in India. Restoration work helped to fill his spare time. This included towers, forts and mosques. He had certain unshakable ideas – when his mind was set, his actions were positive and not open to negotiation. He incurred the wrath of Indians when his renovations to buildings were not the ones requested. He was the sort of architect who would not hesitate to remove the dome off St Paul's Cathedral, if he felt it would look better without it!

Despite such actions, his love for Indian architecture, life and culture developed into an all-consuming passion. However, ill health forced him to leave India so he went to Italy. He then took himself a French wife – he had previously been married to an Indian woman. In keeping with his personality, wild animals freely roamed the gardens of his beautiful, self designed chateau.

In the middle of the nineteenth century, after his wife died, he returned to Devon. His childhood had been spent in Bideford but he, no doubt, thought that his constitution was more suited to the benevolent South Devon climate. So Smith began his 'folly' in 1854. A tower known as 'The Castle' already existed on the site. This had been built in the early nineteenth century as one of many towers built to repel any possible French invasion. Smith encompassed this within his plans.

Apart from the normal standard rooms and fittings, there was an ingenious method of filling a plunge bath. An underground tunnel, direct from the sea, meant that at high tide an invigorating bath could be enjoyed, or endured, as the water gushed in. Colonel Smith must have benefited from his regular cold baths as he survived until he was 86 years old.

Colonel Smith, always a controversial figure, took this quality to the grave, for his inheritance passed to his estranged son in a slightly unusual fashion.

His son had remained in India, after a series of rows between father and son. All links had been severed and the Colonel had no idea of his son's whereabouts. Consequently, when it came to tracing him, the Colonel's solicitors had to put messages in leading newspapers in England and India. Smith Junior had taken up the position of a head waiter in an Indian Hotel, close to an English barracks, which many officers frequented. One of them was reading the 'personal' column and, knowing that the head waiter was called Smith (not an uncommon name), jokingly said: "Is this you, old boy?" It was! Smith Junior, who had struggled on independently, followed this up and became a very wealthy man overnight.

However, because he was poorly educated, and perhaps he had also inherited his father's stubborn streak, he soon spent his inheritance. Typical of his folly was the purchase of a large clock which he saw on a London building. He was so taken by it that he enquired within how much it was. The shop owner was not particularly keen to sell it and asked a grossly inflated price. Thus the 'Gog Magog' clock was installed at Redcliffe.

Young Smith eventually sold the house which, after changing hands a few times, became a hotel in 1902. During the Boer War, Paris Singer sponsored 20 beds at Redcliffe for troops requiring treatment. Now it is a comfortable, well appointed hotel.

There always seems to be plenty happening on Paignton sea front, the Green being ideal for recreation and relaxation. However, in the past it has seen many different activities and once was even regarded as a public nuisance. In the times when Paignton was becoming an attractive place to live, the area of the Green was an extensive area of sand dunes. As the land was developed, this was flattened and lawned out.

One of Paignton's traditional attractions, which has been missed for several seasons, is its donkeys. Earlier this century 'Donkey Daniels', proudly parading his team of donkeys along the shore, gave hundreds of young children a good time. He was often to be seen imbibing from a brown bottle claiming, "tis only cold tea, me dears!" This beverage would not, however, have explained his erratic behaviour; he was frequently seen in a state of inebriation, cheerfully using walls around the town to guide him home. Despite his erring ways, he was a popular figure and regarded as totally harmless by the community.

Another local character, seen all over Paignton in the past, was Granny Symonds, also known as 'Mother Bundles', who scared the wits out of local children by her aggressive manner, raucous voice and frightening appearance. It seems her most unusual trait was the variety of hats that she wore—not one at a time, but many piled high on top of each other!

Anyone who knows Paignton would instantly recognise the distinctly red sands so much a geographical fingerprint of this resort. So they would be flabbergasted to have seen a brochure in 1992 that promoted the resort. This had a striking colourful photograph on its cover showing brilliant *white* sand from some distant shore!

The beaches of Paignton were previously owned by the Duchy of Cornwall who offered the sands to the local board in 1883. The asking price was £220 but this was considered too much. Twenty years later the town got to own their foreshore, Paignton Sands being acquired for £256. It took another decade before Preston Sands were purchased whilst Goodrington Sands were bought in stages, the last not until 1938.

A traditional feature, apparently missing from Paignton sea front, is a bandstand, but Paignton did once have one. The photograph, taken about 1930, shows it almost opposite the junction of Torbay Road, where the Festival Theatre now stands. The local Corporation delved into the realms of fantasy when they looked

for a name for it and, throwing caution to the wind, came up with 'The Bandstand'!

The Bandstand first appeared in 1920. In response to the growing reputation of Paignton as a resort, it underwent frequent modifications. By the time it was ready for demolition, in the 1960s, it had acquired a large dance stage, seating capacity for more than 1,300, attractive ornamental gardens and a different name, 'The Summer Pavilion'. However, sadly outdated, it had to give way to the Festival Theatre which has attracted hundreds of 'big name stars' who would never have agreed to appear at such a humble spot as 'The Bandstand'. The first show put on at the Festival Theatre was The Black and White Ministrels on 10 June 1967.

Peter Randall, proud town crier of Paignton, received a directive from the Torbay Tourism Office to go forth one Sunday morning and proclaim the forthcoming events at Torquay, Paignton and Brixham. At Torquay there was no problem but, at Paignton sea front, poor Peter had a confrontation with a beach inspector, who informed him that he could not ring his bell as it contravened a local byelaw. The town crier was told that he could shout as loudly as he wished, but he could not ring his bell. The solution proposed was that a cardboard cut-out of the bell could be waved instead. This was completely dingless and dongless, but it silenced the beach inspector. This little drama became nationally known when the BBC featured it on *That's Life!*

Paignton can claim, with great pride, the unique distinction of staging the world premiere of a famous operetta. *The Pirates of Penzance* was first performed in the tiniest of theatres imaginable – more or less where the Woolworth's store is now sited near the railway crossing in Paignton's town centre. Here there once stood a hotel called The Gerston. Its owner was Mr Hyde Dendy, and at the back of the premises he had a pocket-sized theatre called the Royal Bijou Theatre. 'Bijou' is French for 'jewel' and the jewel in the crown of this theatre was the hurried production of the *Pirates of Penzance* which was performed on Tuesday 30 December 1879 by a touring D'Oyley Carte company. The costumes for the first performance of *Pirates* included knotted handkerchiefs instead of pirates' hats and instead of being greeting by thousands of ardent fans only 70 specially invited

guests were present on the historic occasion – some of these standing as there were only 50 seats. The reason for the haste and subterfuge was that its creators, Gilbert and Sullivan, had been cheated out of their royalties in America for *HMS Pinafore*. Performed only a matter of weeks earlier in London, carefully planted spies had managed to write down all the music and words at its premiere. These had been rushed across the Atlantic where theatre 'pirates' performed the play before the authors had established copyright. Thus to safeguard their entitlements in future, *The Pirates of Penzance* having been performed in Paignton was immediately shipped to the States. Co-incidentally, in the 1982 film version with Kevin Kline and Linda Ronstadt, Paignton lady Myrtle Devenish had a small part in the crowd scenes at the end of the film.

Sundays were somewhat dull affairs in mid-Victorian Paignton. Demonstrative activity, however well-intentioned, was frowned upon by the strong church-going community. The calm tranquillity and quietude of the resort was, however, rudely interrupted by the Salvation Army, who had their first Paignton HQ at the Harbour. It was felt that their flag waving, drum thumping, noisy form of marching worship, whilst parading across Paignton Green, desecrated the Sabbath! Boisterous opposition was raised in the form of a group called 'the Skeleton Army'. This mob caused much disruption of the Salvation Army processions after they had left the Harbour. They filed in, amidst the ranks, to cause utter chaos. To make matters worse, these unholy persons adopted a pirate-style flag of a skull and crossbones, and proudly traded used the motto 'Beef, Beer and Baccy'.

Another episode of disruption occurred on Paignton Green in mid-Victorian times. For anyone who thinks bizarre events are a recent development dreamed up by the *Guinness Book of Records*, here is one cooked up to whet the appetite of the most discerning palates of outrage!

These are the ingredients for a recipe for just one of the famous Paignton Puddings, produced twice a century for very special occasions: 500 lbs of flour, 190 lbs of bread, 400 lbs of raisins, 184 lbs of currants, 400 lbs of suet, 96 lbs of sugar, 320 lemons and 150 nutmegs. For good measure (or bad if your maths are weak) you need to add a pint of milk for each pound of solid content. This 1859 masterpiece was made in honour of the coming of the railway to Paignton. In 1859 it cost only £45 to make and was scheduled to serve 3,000 invited guests. It was such a large pudding that several horses were required to pull it along on a wagon.

An impressive procession proceeded from Primley to Paignton Green which

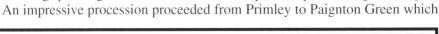

comprised, in order, navvies with their picks and shovels, waiters, a band, a bread wagon (with nearly a ton of bread) pulled by three horses, committee members, the pudding, followed by more committee members, the secretary, the general arrangement committee, a policeman and assorted inhabitants!

At Paignton Green there was an electric atmosphere, thousands of visitors having made the pilgrimage to the town by sea and road. The harbour was 'free' for the day as a special concession. It was estimated that 18,000 were there to spectate and the 3,000 'lucky' ones were seated in a huge circle ready to be served. The carnival atmosphere was generated with plenty of loud music and a variety of entertainments.

Although the newspapers reported that there were no incidents it is known that this was not the case. Despite the fact that five large policemen (who were in no way in need of any pudding themselves) guarded the pudding, the cordon was still broken by an unruly mob. Hand to hand fighting, between the uninvited mass and invited guests, soon broke out. In the chaos a goodly amount of the pudding was grossly misused! Soon the pudding had disappeared.

In the following weeks the post office at Paignton reported that a vast number of greasy packages had been sent abroad – presumably containing fragments, or souvenirs, of the 1859 Paignton Pudding!

But not all the goings on at Paignton Green are as chaotic. Travelling fairs sometimes are permitted to set up shop here and hundreds of people enjoy the thrills, but hopefully not the spills, of the rides. Every year superbly organised firework displays illuminate the night skies above the resort, events which draw thousands in to gaze in wonderment. At such times many people throng the open spaces on the steep hillsides above the town to enjoy the overall spectacle. Such events raise money for charity and prove that Paignton is a live and vibrant seaside town.

Another regular visitor to Paignton is the Radio One FM Roadshow which travels around the country in the summer months. Each show has its star guests and the statistic that it is listened to by millions of people guarantees that whenever it is in town it attracts enormous crowds.

Paignton's Pier has always acted like a  magnet to young people and has an eventful history. In 1871 Mr Dendy started the Bathing Machine Company and the following year he introduced an omnibus service to Torquay. However, his desire to bring a fine pier to Paignton caused

him a few problems. He bought Teignmouth Pier with the intention of dismantling it and reassembling it at Paignton. Unfortunately for Dendy difficulties arose, so he refurbished the pier instead and it reopened in Teignmouth on 24 July 1876. Dendy decided Paignton must have a new pier and by 1879 the new erection was ready. The Pavilion Pier was 780 feet long and at the end of it was the Grand Pavilion which measured 80 feet by 25 feet – room enough to cater for a vast array of entertainments, including dancing and billiards.

Musical performances took place two or three times a day in the summer season and on Sundays, in late Victorian times, organ recitals of religious music and hymns were given. It is hard to imagine that happening on Paignton Pier today — "Eyes down, look in, now let's sing hymn number, all the sixes, 66!" However disaster struck the pier on Thursday 18 June 1919 when a major fire at the seaward end of the pier took hold. The grand piano was set ablaze and plummeted down into the sea along with much of the pier's structure.

Today the reconstructed pier remains a traditional attraction even though its entertainments are vastly different. Should you visit it keep an eye out for the tiny, but nevertheless fascinating, exhibition about the history of piers around our coast. It's well worth a visit, one of the best free shows in town!

Beyond Paignton Harbour a great red sandstone headland – Roundham Head – projects several hundred yards out into the bay, forming a natural divide between the main beach and Goodrington Sands. In Peter Tully's excellent book *Pictures of Paignton Part II* there is a fine photograph taken from the air in the

1920s which shows this distinct feature, an obviously harder and more resistant headland than the surrounding rocks.

To the south of it is Goodrington Park, another of Paignton's many playgrounds. This is a children's paradise with many entertainments to thrill and excite. It is also, however, a most interesting environment because through the years, it has seen plenty of change and a lot of exciting action. It would be all too easy to forget this past in the subtropical gardens of Roundham Head, or whilst entangled with one of those distracting electronic games in Goodrington's amusement park.

If you were to stand on the railway bridge, over the Torbay and Dartmouth railway, and examine the nature of the topography you would notice that the land

was very flat – a low coastal plain extending almost as far as Paignton Zoo, although this is cleverly camouflaged in thick woodland. Much of it has been reclaimed for recreational use with sports pitches and The Torbay Leisure Centre on the site. This aerial photograph looks down on the Grange Court Holiday

Centre. Penwill Way rises on the right side of the photo. In the middle is an area of flat land which has been dammed to create some attractive lakes.

This plain, which accepted the flow of slow moving streams, was poorly drained, in common with other great tracts of land in the Paignton area. It was also a world where a watery wilderness existed, a marshland of little use, or so it seems. A large lagoon, or lake, locally called May's Pool, occupied an area close to the sea. Parents warned their offspring of dire consequences if they fell in the 'bottomless pool'. In 1667 Richard Thorne did his bit to perpetuate the story by drowning there after falling from his horse. Hundreds of years later when Goodrington Park was being reclaimed, it was found that this 'bottomless pool' was all of two feet deep! Now it is a boating pool, still about the same depth.

In Richard Thorne's time smuggling was rampant throughout Torbay. The Paignton smugglers, who landed their goods at Goodrington Sands, were regarded as being at the top of their trade. This was because there were no records of any prosecutions or discoveries of contraband in Paignton, even though it is known that the smugglers were very active.

In researching tales of smuggling one tends to find that the same old tales crop up, time after time, at almost every coastal location. A favourite is the use of a funeral procession to act as a cover. A procession with muffled hooves and a

coffin, bearing a different sort of spirit to the one expected, was commonplace at Goodrington. To substantiate this story there was a funeral route which went from Goodrington to Paignton, via Knapp Park Lane, along the beach through Young's Park, along Midvale and Palace Avenues to the churchyard. It seems that this was often done at night and, to create a sense of presence, the horses' heads were daubed with phosphorescent paint. Strangely, when a plague was raging, Paignton remained almost unaffected, whilst the population of Goodrington was decimated.

In Goodrington Park there is a lone grave which puzzles curious visitors. 'The Major's Grave' has a granite headstone with a simple inscription. Goodrington

CLIFF GARDENS, GOODRINGTON.

Park was consecrated ground – a significant fact which helps to dismiss the theory that this is the grave of a suicide victim. In fact it might be the only headstone, but it is not the only grave – the remains of three hundred French sailors reputedly lie beneath the park. A convent of Roman Catholic nuns cared for French prisoners of war at this spot. The Major was supposedly killed in action but because he was

English he had the privilege of a head-stone and marked grave. Variations of the story occur.

During the Napoleonic wars there were many incidents in and around Torbay. On the night of 24 October 1804, HMS *Venerable* went aground on Paignton Ledge, a shallow shelf of rock extending out from Roundham Head. Three men were lost overboard but most of the 555 crew got off safely.

The Goodrington we know today began to emerge in 1929. Funds from the 'distressed arms relief scheme' enabled an army of imported Welsh men to embark on a project designed to strengthen and beautify Roundham Head. By 1931, 80,000 tons of sandstone had been moved in an attempt to prevent coastal erosion. The zig-zag paths which weave across the headland looked raw and stark so Herbert Whitley kindly provided many subtropical plants, shrubs and trees to heal the scars and create some lovely surroundings. There was a proposal to call these grounds the Alexander Gardens after the First Lord of the Admiralty who had a tenuous connection with Paignton. However a change of government resulted in this idea being abandoned. By 1935 the park, on what some people called Paradise Head, was laid out in fine ornamental fashion – a site of "verdure, floral and aquatic splendour".

The mile of coastline between Goodrington and Broadsands is a somewhat untidy one. The developers, balked by the railway line, have done their best to encroach upon the sea.

The rambler passing along this coastal stretch, will notice that, for what appears to be a low coastline, there seems to be a lot of steps up and down. Sugar Loaf Hill is not as sweet on the feet as it sounds. The footpath stays on the urban landward side of the railway until Waterside is reached, then the railway can be crossed for more natural surroundings. Slightly to the north of this is Saltern Cove, a rocky nature reserve where children can spend hours delving into rock-pools.

The geologist can also find much of interest in this immediate area. The complex formation of the rocks is best noted in the great diversity of rock types appearing. Mudstones, limestones and volcanic beds all outcrop (appear at the surface) together. Armchair Rock is an isolated stack, whilst the coastal cliffs are volcanic in origin. However it is a little further to the south that the most impressive spectacle occurs – The Crystal Cave. The cave is webbed with a mass of calcite veins, which results in every wall glittering with millions of small crystals. There is a natural temptation to collect a few souvenirs (geological vandalism), but it is better to settle for an unusual photograph and the memory of its great beauty.

The short distance to Broadsands is covered by a well defined path, which rises yet again before falling back down to sea level. As its name suggests, Broadsands has broad sands (when the tide is out). There is a large car park which again has been built on reclaimed marsh land. This photograph was taken before it was

built. Some of it survives by the small stream which flows into the sea. It is a popular spot and has facilities normally associated with a day out on the beach. Film makers have been here at various times. There was a Jim'll Fix It sequence shot here of a young girl fulfilling her wish to ride a horse in the sea – thereby bringing a new interpretation to what constitutes a sea horse. Gabrielle Drake and comedian Kelly Monteith did some sketches for the latter's show. John Cleese arrived with the Monty Python team to shoot a series of sketches with the scantily dressed Carol Cleveland. You may recall him sat at an office desk whilst the waves broke all around him. There are more details of these stories in the book *Made in Devon*.

There is a pleasant walk on along the low cliffs of Elberry on to Brixham but that is continued in our Brixham book.

All along the Paignton coastline it has been possible to hear the not so distant sound of trains rumbling along. One way or another the railways have been a major influence on the town, even down to its name ...

During Paignton's long, mostly dignified history the spelling of the settlement's name has varied greatly. There have been no less than thirty variations. This of course is not peculiar only to Paignton because places such as Dawlish and Cullompton have also experienced many changes in name. However, the two variations which rivalled each other during the Victorian era were Paignton and Paington. Locals were divided about the spelling and some signs used one variation whereas others used the alternative. The situation was not helped when a railway surveyor, who quizzed locals, was equally convinced by both factions. As a result both versions appeared on the railway map! His indecision was also evident at the station where each platform bore different spellings. Throughout the following years this caused much consternation to visitors and created a lot of head scratching. It was resolved when a newly appointed Stationmaster was appalled at the inconsistency and contacted the local postmaster who preferred 'Paignton'. Ever since this spelling has predominated.

Every summer, thousands of people take advantage of the steam line from Paignton to Kingswear. A nostalgic journey, on a yesteryear form of transport, awaits the traveller. For the connoisseur of scenery, there can be few railway rides to match the variety, and beauty, found along the line to Kingswear.

The journey begins, for most, at Paignton. In the past Paignton had expresses arriving every few minutes, to keep the Goodrington sidings busy. Those days have long gone, the endless queues of traffic into Torbay bearing testimony to the changing pattern of transport use.

The Torbay and Dartmouth Railway have their own station at Paignton, with all the necessary facilities to run independently from British Rail, although 'big brother' has jurisdiction over the first few hundred metres of line towards Goodrington.

Steep gradients on the line mean that powerful locomotives are needed. Beyond Goodrington, the line climbs for 2½ miles to Churston, with gradients up to 1:60 – steep for railway engines. The seaward views are striking, specially from the two towering viaducts, Hookhills and Broadsands.

Churston is on the watershed, the great divide between Torbay and the lower Dart Valley. From here the railway drops alarmingly to the Dart estuary, with gradients as steep as 1:66. The hilly topography meant that the railway engineers were reduced to creating deep cuttings, high embankments, viaducts and Greenway Tunnel. The latter is nearly 500 yards long and marks a change from open pastoral countryside to a heavily wooded landscape. Within minutes the railway reaches the Dart. On one side the estuary shimmers and bustles with activity, whilst on the other an impenetrable forest rises sharply up above the railway.

This was *Onedin Line* country. It was not intended to be Devon, but the Amazon Jungle. The film makers often started a 'take', using the dense forest as a jungle backcloth, only to find puffs of smoke billowing up from the passing steam trains. There was also a lot of locational filming of the *French Lieutenant's Woman* at Kingswear, this station playing the part of Exeter in the adaptation of John Fowles' novel.

The six mile journey is a classic way to savour the Torbay landscape.

Beside Paignton Station is a fine cinema which is owned and run by the steam railway. This grand old cinema, opened in 1914, has the distinction of being the first purpose-built cinema in the West Country. It remains the only one in the town and, despite the closure, demolition or change of function of other picture palaces, this one lives on with great optimism.

The cinema is haunted by the ghost of a previous owner. He loved a certain unusual but distinctive type of tobacco. The unmistakable aroma of the pipe smoke often can be detected by staff when the cinema is empty. Donald Sutherland shot a scene from the film *Ordeal By Innocence* in the balcony here but when he runs out from the cinema he exits from a cinema in Dartmouth! The latter has since been demolished. The Torbay Cinema's balcony was more than strong enough to take the weight of all the great movie cameras. When the cinema was built, its architect had never seen a cinema before and was concerned as to whether the balcony was up to the job. Therefore, many strong men were invited along to sit through a film show with a hundredweight bag of sand on their laps! Fortunately the balcony was well able to stand the weight.

As we have already seen, most of the Paignton flat lands were marshy swamps reclaimed in the latter half of the nineteenth century. Queens Park, a delightful retreat from the glare of loud gift shops, was also a marsh. As a wasteland it became frequented by gypsies, showmen, and all manner of drifting travellers. Its poor reputation assured it priority for reclamation when it came to making Paignton a wholesome and civilised environment.

Palace Avenue has a classy look about it, with superior buildings, and attractive, dog-free public gardens, in a fashionable corner of Paignton. However, it is not too long ago that it was referred to as 'Withy-Platts' as it was just a watery wilderness. Large numbers of willow trees and withies grew in abundance. This provided a considerable source for local basket makers, and those who made crab pots. Little girls made pocket money by gathering the wild camomile which was made into wine or tea, whilst little boys collected leeches for local doctors.

The Paignton area was noted for the vast areas of orchards that clothed the hillsides around Yalberton, Shorton and Marldon. Thousands of gallons of cider were shipped to London and Dublin each year. On the lower, more fertile soils, the legendary Paignton cabbage was grown in such proliferation that vast amounts were sold to distant markets. There were two main types of cabbages: the flat-pole which was best suited for animal feed as it was somewhat earthy; the other type being much sweeter and tastier – the local population had the good sense to consume the bulk of the latter. There was quite an export market for the flat-pole to Norway, where it would seem that their taste in cabbages was as good as their ability to write Eurovision songs! (For the uninitiated, Norway has the dubious distinction of scoring "nil points" on several occasions.)

No book about Paignton would be complete without a mention of its main tourist attraction ... Paignton Zoo.

Herbert Whitley was a wealthy recluse whose main passion was adding to his personal menagerie. He travelled extensively, and even had the honour of having a bird named after him – Whitley's Conure. Mr Whitley's collection became too large for the grounds of his 'Primley' home, so he earmarked another part of his estate, on the opposite side of the Totnes Road, as a zoological garden.

Around 1922/23 was a busy time, as the construction of aviaries, dens, cattle sheds, and the laying out of the grounds, required a lot of work. The grounds were opened without ceremony, but Primley Zoo fell foul of the Tax Man, who insisted that 'Amusement Tax' should be included in the admission price. Mr Whitley flatly refused to collect the tax so, in March 1924, was taken to court.

Mr Whitley responded to the judgment against him by closing the gardens to the public. At the entrances an explanatory notice was pinned up. He felt that his zoo was educational, not entertainment, and he did not intend to defraud the public by charging tax where no entertainment existed.

His collection of flora and fauna continued to grow at such an alarming rate that, in June 1927, he was obliged to swallow his pride and re-open the zoo, amusement tax and all. Since then Primley Zoo, now Paignton Zoological and Botanical Gardens, has blossomed into an established venue. Paignton's 1948 Guide Book relates that "the Gardens are a worthy challenge to Regents Park and Kew", whilst the overall contribution to the resort is summed up, "This galaxy of novelty is an amazing seaside amenity".

Zoological Gardens, Paignton

The zoo's history has been fairly tame, but one episode which caused much alarm involved a leopard called Ben.

Zoos are a bit like prisons in that if a dangerous inmate escapes there is chaos. In January 1939, the national papers had headlines about the escape of a leopard from Paignton Zoo, but most of the locals took it very calmly. The incident began when the leopard mauled his keeper, Mr Jack Hawkins, before making off into the densely vegetated grounds. It transpired that the leopard never actually left the zoo, but there were still many sitings, like in a linhay at White Rock Farm, the location of the 1937 Devon County Show, and at Goodrington. At White Rock Farm, in the dark, a search party had a muddy time squelching around fruitlessly as the rain poured down mercilessly. The following day, a former Canadian Mounted Policeman, Major Yorke, eventually found himself just a few metres from the seven-year-old Indian leopard, which crouched motionless, almost indistinguishable amidst the heavy undergrowth. The order had been to take it dead or alive but Major Yorke, under instruction from Inspector Hutchings, killed it in one shot. It was reported that the leopard's skin was to be mounted and presented to Major Yorke.

Today Paignton Zoo has to battle for its own survival, in a climate which has proven too harsh for other Devonshire zoos, like Exmouth and Plymouth. In its defence, its large animal collection, botanical gardens, tropical houses, library and classrooms provide a great number of schoolchildren, and students, with an educational experience which they will always remember. The Devon Zoology Centre, based in the Zoo, gives school and college groups, from the county, inexpensive access to these extensive facilities.

In normal circumstances one would not list the council offices of the local corporation as a place for the holidaymakers to visit – but in Paignton it is highly recommended. In Oldway Manor the local council has a prized asset of great beauty and a history which encompasses many household names.

Isaac Merritt Singer was born in New York, the son of a German father and Dutch mother. His parents lived in abject poverty, and died equally impoverished, when Isaac was still young. He was a bright lad, willing to try almost anything to earn a living. After a spell of farming, and a brief acting career, he turned his attention to engineering. It was not until he was 41 years old, and married for the second time, that he made a breakthrough, by producing a working sewing machine which could be manufactured in great volume.

In 1871, Singer was aware that life in his adopted France was in danger of total disruption so, with his beautiful wife Isabella, and their young family, moved to South Devon. His first purchase was the Fernham Estate, which consisted two villas, Little Oldway and Fernham, the Rising Sun Inn, some cottages and a substantial area of parkland. The Rising Sun sank, as did the cottages, when they were pulled down as part of an elaborate plan.

As well as being rich, Isaac was an imaginative man. He employed local architect, George Bridgman, to build him a large edifice that he planned to call 'The Wigwam'. Even though France is not known for its Red Indians, Singer sent

Bridgman there to ascertain certain details. Bridgman may well have had his 'reservations', but he complied with Singer's instructions. By 1874 Bridgman had created a magnificent building, containing kitchens, offices, servants hall, wine cellars, many fine rooms and even a theatre, which resembled a florid French villa. Alas, poor Isaac died just before the mansion was completed.

The man born into poverty left an immense fortune of 13 million dollars, plus a vast estate – from humble rags to well stitched ones. Perhaps his greatest legacies, though, were his six children, Mortimer, Washington, Winnaretta, Paris, Isabella and Franklin (Adam), plus his great love of all children. Before his death, he treated every child in Paignton to a visit to a travelling show, and he had his butlers stationed at the gates, ready to dish out a bag of sweets to each one as they left afterwards.

Isaac Singer's widow eventually went back to Paris where her good looks attracted much attention. Celebrated sculptor Auguste Bartholdi was just one admirer. He persuaded Isabella to model for him. The end result is perhaps the most famous statue in the world – The Statue of Liberty!

The Wigwam remained almost unaltered, until 1904 when Isaac's third son, Paris, began a series of major alterations. The house was renamed Oldway after the changes, but many people called it The Little Versailles, because of the great similarity the redesigned building had to its French equivalent. The Gallery was modelled on The Hall of Mirrors at Versailles, whilst the music pavilion was based on one from the grounds of The Petit Trianon, also at Versailles. The vast team of craftsmen, and artists, had the bulk of the work finished by 1907. Happily, a vast amount of the work they did remains on view today.

The use of Oldway as a family residence was short lived. At the outset of the First World War, Paris Singer personally funded the adaptation of the manor to an American Women's War Hospital. Hospital trains full of wounded soldiers

soon arrived at Paignton. The local fire brigade stretchered the patients to the house. Ironically, more American troops died there as a result of a 'flu epidemic, than from wounds, and were buried in Paignton. Following the war, their bodies were taken back to the USA.

After the war, the house ceased to be used as a family home, although a few rooms were fitted up as a flat, for occasional occupation by the Singers, several of whom remained in the Paignton area.

In 1929 the property became the Torbay Country Club. The ground floor was re-organised to include a cafe, billiards rooms, a bar and toilets. The upper floors were converted into residential flats. Outside two bowling greens and fifteen tennis courts provided extra facilities. The RAF requisitioned several of Oldway's buildings during the Second World War, using them for the Initial Training Wing. Paignton's council took possession after the war and got, what must be, the absolute bargain of the century, when they purchased it for only £45,000.

But what of the many Singers? The most romantic story surrounds Paris, who fell in love with the legendary dancer, Isadora Duncan. His courtship of her, in 1909, was graphically dramatised in a film called *Isadora*. Many shots and scenes were filmed in and around Oldway. Vanessa Redgrave played the title role, ably supported by Jason Robards Junior (see *Made in Devon*).

Mortimer and Franklin Singer were both fond of the sea and spent a lot of time on maritime pursuits. Washington Singer was a famous racehorse owner – one of his horses won the prestigious St Leger. Isaac and Isabella's two daughters both married into foreign Royal families. Isabella became Duchess De Cazes whilst Winnaretta, who was a talented musician and artist, became Princess de Polignnac.

The lovely theatre created by Isaac Singer became a ballroom when Paris Singer took command, and latterly has become the council chamber. Film stars, the wealthy elite, kings and queens, members of NALGO, and tourists, are only a small cross section of the vast number of people who have worked rested or played at The Wigwam or Oldway. Go and have a look around the gardens, they are gorgeous!

And so it is then that we come to the end of our brief but selective look at just some of the events from Paignton's past. If you were one of those people who thought Paignton is 'just another seaside town' then we hope this has helped to change your mind and encouraged you to look at the town from a different angle. If it has whetted your appetite to learn more about Paignton's past then we heartily recommend Peter Tully's two books of *Pictures of Paignton*, collections of old photographs which can often say so much more than mere words ever can.